ON THE
SITE OF THE GLOBE PLAYHOUSE
OF SHAKESPEARE

Objects found on the site of 6 and 7 Bankside

ON THE
SITE OF THE GLOBE PLAYHOUSE
OF SHAKESPEARE

LYING TO THE NORTH OF MAIDEN LANE,
BANKSIDE, SOUTHWARK

BY

GEORGE HUBBARD, F.S.A.
VICE-PRESIDENT R.I.B.A.

"Sweet Swan of Avon! What a sight it were
To see thee in our waters yet appear
And make those flights upon the Banks of Thames
That so did take Eliza and our James."

BEN JONSON *First Folio*

CAMBRIDGE
AT THE UNIVERSITY PRESS
1923

CAMBRIDGE
UNIVERSITY PRESS

University Printing House, Cambridge CB2 8BS, United Kingdom

Cambridge University Press is part of the University of Cambridge.

It furthers the University's mission by disseminating knowledge in the pursuit of
education, learning and research at the highest international levels of excellence.

www.cambridge.org
Information on this title: www.cambridge.org/9781316605516

© Cambridge University Press 1923

First published 1923
First paperback edition 2016

A catalogue record for this publication is available from the British Library

ISBN 978-1-316-60551-6 Paperback

PREFACE

THERE has been considerable uncertainty concerning the site of the Globe Theatre since Parliamentary times, but opinion gravitated towards the site of Barclay and Perkins' Brewery, until Prof. Wallace discovered the lawsuit between Thomasina Ostler and her father John Hemynges, and published it in 1909. That gives clear details of the property, the exact boundaries of the leasehold, and a rough plan of the holdings of the previous tenants. It was certainly to the *North* of Maiden Lane, whereas the Brewery Site lies to the South. Much correspondence ensued, as one party of critics boldly assumed that, as there was *no Park* to the North, the plan used in the lawsuit was wrong in its orientation, and had to be "turned upside down." As I had proved there *was* a place called "the Park" to the North, and as all contemporary evidence of manuscript, print and maps harmonized with the legal testimony, I was preparing a pamphlet, to answer those who accepted the topsy-turvy arrangement. The Shakespeare Reading Society affixed a Bronze tablet in 1913 on Barclay and Perkins' Brewery wall affirming that the site lay there. I appealed to the London County Council in that year, but they took no notice. I appealed again in 1921, and they issued an "Official pamphlet" confirming the site of the Brewery Tablet. A friend, in whose judgment I could rely, advised me that my arguments would have more extensive hearing if issued in book form, than in pamphlet form. Hence I have produced this little volume containing my arguments, fortified by a long series of Map Views (though the County Council pamphlet ignores all these). I felt that I owed it to posterity to preserve the testimony of 16th Century witnesses and contemporary research.

GEORGE HUBBARD.

January 1923.

ILLUSTRATIONS

OBJECTS FOUND ON THE SITE OF 6 AND 7 BANKSIDE.   *Frontispiece*

PLATES

ON THE
SITE OF THE GLOBE PLAYHOUSE
OF SHAKESPEARE

FOR a long period there has been considerable uncertainty and diversity of opinion as to the exact site of the Globe Playhouse. The solution of the question may not be a matter of vast importance to anyone: but, in view of the fact that the Shakespeare Reading Society has erected a large bronze memorial to commemorate the site, and that the London County Council have published an official document which purports to settle the question, the matter assumes a certain importance which it would not otherwise have had.

During the centuries that have passed since the Globe was demolished in 1644 all the surrounding property has been pulled down, the ownerships of the sites have been transferred, and now such papers as remain concerning the transactions are too frequently neglected.

In this century new material has been found, including contemporary documents, from which data are available for the more exact determination of the site.

The students of our time, however, do not always read and understand these, as they were intended to be read and understood. In our search after truth it is necessary to bring together and compare the printed and manuscript testimonies, which are at the present time available, and to compare these with the long series of map views of the period. The truth is not beyond our reach if we are content to accept the evidence without prejudice.

We must begin with the contemporary documents, as these afford the most reliable evidence, and, in the absence of definite proof of error, they must be accepted in preference to later documents, when the two are not in accord.

The question at issue is whether the Globe Playhouse stood to the north or south of a lane then known as Maiden or Maid Lane; but which today is known as Park Street, Southwark. Park Street for the most part runs east and west, roughly parallel with a narrow roadway known as Bankside on the shores of the Thames.

The land lying between Park Street on the south, and Bankside on the north is only about 180 feet deep at its eastern end, where it abuts upon Bank End, a road which used to be known as "Deadman's Place," and at its western end, close by Southwark Bridge, it is about 290 feet deep.

On the south side of Park Street lies the great Brewery of Messrs Barclay Perkins and Co. Ltd. It stands on the ground which formerly was a portion of the Lord Bishop of Winchester's Park.

Did the Globe stand between Maiden Lane and Bankside or did it stand on any portion of the Brewery site? Ben Jonson in *An Execration of Vulcan* says:

> ....The Globe, the glory of the Bank:
> Which, though it were the fort of the whole parish,
> Flank'd with a ditch, and forced out of a marish,
> I saw with two poor chambers taken in,
> And razed; ere thought could urge this might have been!
> See the World's ruins! nothing but the piles
> Left, and wit since to cover it with tiles.

Now Ben Jonson was a precisian in language, and he knew what he was talking about. These words of the poet "the Globe, the glory of the Bank" would hardly be applicable, if the theatre stood some distance away to the south of Maiden Lane, and, some 400 or 500 feet away from the Bank[1], where he says it stood as "though it were the fort of the whole parish."

Moreover this site south of Maiden Lane could only have been approached by a narrow passage way, and, as the chief patrons probably came from the north side of the river they would not appreciate having to

[1] See Note 5, p. 44.

tramp down Deadman's Place with its great sewer in the centre, or along Maiden Lane, which was flanked by a ditch or open sewer on either side, or alternatively along a narrow passage way, before arriving at the theatre. Nor does this seem to convey the idea of a great object, seen from afar, " and gloriously seen " on the Bank.

It was not until Dr Charles William Wallace made the great discovery in the Coram Rege Roll (1454, 13 Jas. 1, Hil. m. 692) dated 1616, which in future will be here referred to as " The Osteler Document," that a contemporary statement, defining the site of the Globe, was brought forward. A full account of this deed, together with a translation of it, by Dr C. W. Wallace, appears in *The Times* of 2nd and 4th October, 1909, and I take the liberty of quoting freely from it, just extracting such facts as bear upon the subject without confining myself to a verbatim quotation.

Dr Wallace points out that this document has reference to family differences leading to a lawsuit. The complainant is Thomasina Osteler, a young widow of 19 years. She was the daughter of John Hemyngs, who had been a close friend of Shakespeare, and later, was one of the co-editors, with Henry Condell, of the famous 1623 folio of Shakespeare's Works.

For Thomasina to make out her case and establish her legal rights, her attorney found it necessary to recount from legal documents, then extant, the history of the shares she claimed in the Globe and Blackfriars Theatres. Although this case is directed against John Hemyngs, it is, in effect, against Shakespeare, the Burbages and the whole Company of Shareholders. Her father, Hemyngs, was included, as he was acting as the business manager and agent of the Company.

The case was probably settled out of Court for there is no judgment recorded.

The extract from the Osteler complaint, which I give in Dr Wallace's translation of the Law-Court Latin of the document, recounts the boundaries of the land, as set out in the original lease, which was granted by Nicholas Brend in 1598–9 to Cuthbert and Richard Burbage, William

Shakespeare, John Hemyngs, Augustine Phillips, Thomas Pope and William Kemp.

That whereas one Nicholas Brend of West Moulsey in the County of Surrey, Esquire, by his indenture tripartite, bearing date the twenty-first day of February in the year of the reign of the Lady Elizabeth, recently Queen of England, the forty-first (1599), for considerations in the same indenture tripartite mentioned and expressed, did demise, grant, and to farm let to those certain men, Cuthbert Burbage and Richard Burbage, of London, gentlemen, to the forementioned William Shakespeare and to Augustine Phillips, and Thomas Pope of London, gentlemen, deceased, to the aforesaid John Hemyngs, and to William Kempe, recently of London, gentleman, deceased, all that parcel of ground just recently before enclosed and made into four separate garden plots recently in the tenure and occupation of Thomas Burt and Isbrand Morris, diers, and of Lactantius Roper, salter, citizen of London, containing in length from east to west two hundred and twenty feet of assize or thereabouts, lying and adjoining upon a way or lane there on one (i.e. south) side and abutting upon a piece of land called The Park upon the north and upon a garden then or recently in the tenure or occupation of one John Cornishe towards the west and upon another garden plot then or recently in the tenure or occupation of one John Knowles towards the east with all the houses, buildings, structures, ways, easements, commodities, and appurtenances thereunto belonging or in any manner pertaining: which said premises are situate, lying, and being within the parish of Saint Saviour in Southwark in the County of Surrey: And also all that parcel of land just recently before enclosed and made into three separate plots whereof two of the same (were) recently in tenure or occupation of John Roberts, carpenter, and another recently in the occupation of one Thomas Ditcher, citizen and merchant tailor, of London, situate, lying, and being in the parish aforesaid in the foresaid county of Surrey, containing in length from east to west by estimation one hundred and fifty-six feet of assize or thereabouts and in breadth from North to South one hundred feet of assize by estimation or thereabouts; lying and adjoining upon the other side of the way or lane aforesaid, and abutting upon a garden plot there then or recently just before in the occupation of William Sellers towards the east, and upon one other garden plot there then or recently just before in the tenure of John Burgram, sadler, towards the west, and upon a lane there, called Maiden Lane, towards the South; with all the houses, buildings, structures, ways, easements, commodities and appurtenances to the last recited premises or to any part or parcel thereof belonging or in any manner pertaining, together with free ingress, egress, and regress, and passage to and fro for the said Cuthbert Burbage and Richard Burbage and to the forementioned William Shakespeare, Augustine Phillips, Thomas Pope, John Hemyngs and William Kemp, their executors, administrators, and assigns, and to all and every other person or persons having occasion to come to them by or through the foresaid way or lane, lying and being between the premises aforesaid, mentioned to be demised as in aforesaid...upon which particular premises, or upon some part thereof, a certain playhouse, suitable for showing forth & acting of comedies and tragedies, did exist.

I have prepared a plan to agree with the particulars given in the Osteler Document, but it is not contended that the four garden plots on the north side of the Way or Lane, or the three garden plots on the south of it, are correctly placed on the plan.

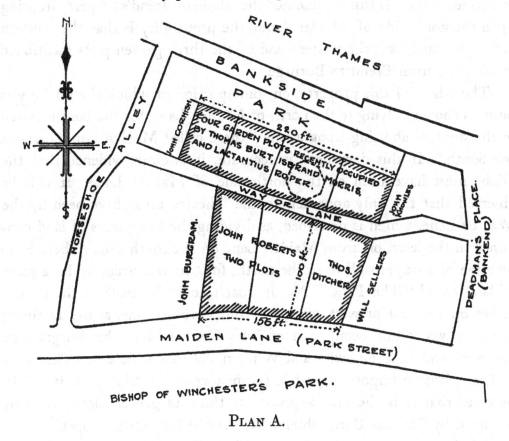

PLAN A.

It is a curious fact that boundaries to parcels of land have a remarkable power of endurance. Thus the depth of the three plots on the south side of the Way or Lane is given as 100 feet. This distance coincides with the long straight boundary, running east and west, between the properties now fronting upon Bankside on the north, and those fronting on Park Street on the south. It therefore in all probability was the southern side of the Way or Lane.

The divisions of the garden plots generally conform to the dividing walls of existing properties; but in assuming the position of the three garden plots fronting on Maiden Lane I have been guided by the fact (as will appear later) that Brend sold land to Memprise having Deadman's Place as its eastern boundary and a frontage of 270 feet on the north side of Maiden Lane. If this represented the whole of Brend's property fronting upon the north side of Maiden Lane, the probability is that the western end of his land, was the western end of the three garden plots mentioned in the lease from Brend to Burbage.

The whole of this property, on some portion of which the Globe was built, is shown as lying to the north of Maiden Lane, for the land is stated in the deed as abutting upon a lane " there called Maiden Lane, towards the South." If this document is accurate, it is clear evidence that the Globe must have been on the north side of Maiden Lane. It will be observed that the only approach to the Theatre must have been by the Way or Lane, which is described, as dividing the two pieces of land contained in the lease, or, from Maiden Lane on the south side. There is no mention of an approach from the north, for this was occupied by a piece of land called " The Park." No approach could be made to the theatre either on the east or west, except by the Way or Lane, as the adjoining property was in the occupation of John Cornish and John Burgram on the west, and John Knowles and William Sellers on the east. This Way or Lane plays an important part in the history of the Globe, and it will be observed that it is the only approach to the four garden plots " recently occupied by Thomas Burt, Isbrand Morris and Lactantius Roper."

We have now a certain amount of local knowledge as to the position of the site of the Globe Playhouse ; but this is by no means complete.

We have certain measurements given to us; but there is no measurement from any fixed point, which can be recognised today. No doubt at the time, with complete local information, it would have been possible to identify the site from the descriptions given. Fortunately, apart from the Osteler document, certain topographical details can be added.

Strype, in his edition of Stow's *Survey*, 1720, says:

Maiden Lane, a long straggling place with ditches on each side, the passage to the houses being built over little bridges, with little garden plots before them, especially on the North side which is best for houses and inhabitants.

This scrap of information is interesting, and, it becomes a matter of high importance, when it is realized that the occupiers or owners of the land fronting upon these sewers, or open ditches, were responsible for their proper maintenance. In this water-logged land which must have been repeatedly flooded by the Spring tides in the Thames it became necessary for Southwark to found a Sewers Commission.

In the *Report on Local Records* (1901, p. 273) compiled by the late Sir Laurence Gomme, Statistical Officer of the London County Council, it appears that the oldest Sewer Commission was The Surrey and Kent Commission of Sewers, instituted under the Act of Henry VIII in the year 1514–15. The earliest existing volume is dated Jan. 1568–9.

In *The Times*, 30th April, 1914, Dr Wallace points out that on the 14th Feb. 1605, the Sewer Commission made the following minute:

It is ordered that Burbage & Heminges and the other owners of the Playhouse called the Globe in Maid Lane shall......pull up and take cleane out of the sewer the props and posts which stand under theire bridge on the North side of Mayd Lane.

It would be difficult to imagine a better piece of cross evidence proving that the Globe Playhouse was on the north side of Maiden Lane.

The Osteler document tells us that the land on which the Globe was built abutted upon Maiden Lane towards the south. Strype tells us that there were two ditches, one on either side of Maiden Lane. As Maiden

Lane ran east and west there was one ditch on the north side, and one on the south side of the lane.

And now by a Minute of the Sewers Commission we are told that the lessees, Burbage and Hemyngs and the other owners of the Playhouse called the Globe, are to carry out certain works *under their bridge on the north side of Maid Lane.*

This cumulative evidence coming from quite independent sources, is, in itself, conclusive on the main point at issue, as to whether the Globe was on the north or the south side of Maiden Lane. If further evidence is required the case of William Sellers might be quoted.

On the 5th Dec. 1595, that is four years before the lease was granted by Nicholas Brend to the brothers Burbage, Shakespeare and others, the Sewer Commissioners ordered

John Warden, and Willm. Sellers and all the land-holders or their tenants that holde anie landes, gardeins, ground or tenements abutting upon the common sewer leading from Sellers' gardein to the beare gardein, to cast, clense and scowre &c.

The Bear garden was on the north side of Maiden Lane, and, therefore, presumably Sellers was on the north side, otherwise his land would have drained into the sewer on the south side of Maiden Lane, and not into the sewer which drained the land on which the Bear garden stood. This evidence that Sellers was on the north side is confirmed by the fact that he is mentioned in the Osteler deed, as adjoining the piece of land granted in the lease. The garden of William Sellers lies to the east of the southern piece of land which was abutting upon Maiden Lane towards the south. Thus there are three documents showing that the site abutted on the north side of Maiden Lane, viz.

1. The Osteler transcript says so.

2. The Minute of the Sewers Commission, 14th Feb. 1605, requests the Globe lessees to remove the props and posts *under their bridge on the north side of Maid Lane.*

3. The Minute of the Sewers Commission, 5th Dec. 1595, shows that Sellers' garden was on the north side of the lane, because it was on the

same side as the Bear Garden, and as, by the Osteler document, he adjoined the Globe site, both his garden and the Globe site must have been on the north side of Maiden Lane.

It now becomes necessary to produce evidence that there was some land known as " The Park " which formed the northern boundary of the piece of land, which is defined clearly in the Osteler complaint. Again we may turn to the evidence contained in the minutes of the Sewer Commissioners.

By reference to the rough plan on page 5 which is drawn to accord with the particulars given in the Osteler document, it will be seen that there are four garden plots abutting upon a piece of land called " The Park " on the north. The names of three of the original occupiers of the gardens are given, Thomas Burt, Isbrand Morris and Lactantius Roper. The only approach to these gardens was from the Way or Lane mentioned in the Osteler document, the back of the gardens would therefore be at the opposite ends of the plots where they abutted upon the piece of land called " The Park " on the north.

On 6th July, 1593, the Commissioners make the following entry:

We present Jasper Morris of London, dyer, to pull up his encroachmente made att the back of his garden into the sewer between his garden and the parck.

On the same date the Commissioners

present Thomas Burt dyer to pull upp his encroachmt. made upon the back of his garden and the parck.

This evidence corroborates what we are told about the Park being on the north as mentioned in the Osteler document and it comes from an entirely independent source. In this case also there are three independent sources of information showing that the site abutted upon a piece of land called the Park on the north. The first being the Osteler document itself, and the other two being the extracts from the minutes of the Sewer Commissioners of 6th July, 1593. As there are very divergent views held in respect to this piece of land called " The Park " any evidence, however small, is worth recording. I therefore quote from a letter I contributed to *The Times* of 3rd Dec. 1921 on this subject.

A paper now at Dulwich College, but which formerly belonged to Edward Alleyn, and afterwards passed on to Malone is quoted in Collier's *Memoirs of Edward Alleyn*. The document is 'a brief noat taken out of the poores booke containing the names of all the inhabitants of the Liberty (the Clink) Wch are rated and assessed to a weekeley paimt. towards the relief of the poore as it stands now increased this 6th day of April 1609 Delivered up to Philip Henslowe Esquior, churchwarden, by Francis Carter, one of the overseers of the same Liberty.'

The list begins as follows:

'Phillip Henslowe Esquior assessed at weekely vid.

Ed. Alleyn assessed at weekely....................vid.

Then follows a list of names, with diminishing amounts as poor rates. The real interest, however, centres around the 28th and 29th names on the list.

The 28th stands as follows: 'Mr Stock for halfe the parke ii^d' and the 29th name 'Hughe Robbinson for halfe the parke ii^d.' This reference to a park, where two men are each assessed at 2d. per week for half the park, could hardly apply to the Lord Bishop of Winchester's park, some 50 or 60 acres, which was by far the greatest individual holding in the Liberty. The question now arises, if this poor rate of 4d. per week did not apply to the Bishop's park, then where is the park in the Liberty of the Clink, to which it could apply? A satisfactory answer to this question can, we think, be made now for the first time.

By reference to the Sacramental Token Books in Southwark Cathedral, the names of the inhabitants are given under the addresses from which the tokens were collected. In the Sacramental Token Books for Bankside in the year 1609 Hugh Robinson's name appears under the sub-heading 'Fro the Parke.' As Hugh Robinson appears to have lived on a piece of land known as the Park, Bankside, on which he paid 2d. per week as a poor rate, it is clear that there was a piece of land known as the Park on Bankside, and this park was, in all probability, the park which formed the northern boundary of the land leased by Brand to Burbage, Shakespeare and others. The deed or lease transcript of 1616 says that 'the land abutted upon a piece of land called the Park on the north...and on the lane there called Maiden Lane towards the South.' This reference to the Park in the Sacramental Token Books ceases in the year 1616 and in no case are there more than three names mentioned under the sub-heading 'Fro the Parke.' It seems unnecessary to labour the point further. These various cross references from distinct and independent sources, do clearly establish the fact that there was a piece of land called 'The Park' which lay to the North of the land leased by Brend to Burbage.

There is complete agreement amongst all the documents which have been referred to up to this point, and so far as I know, there are no contemporary authorities which refute their accuracy.

The evidence of the site of the Globe Playhouse does not rest only on the testimony of the manuscript documents. There are the map-views which tell us graphically exactly what the deeds tell us literally.

Maps as we understand them today are plans of buildings or streets drawn to a small scale. The distance between the buildings and the length of the streets can be measured; but this accurate form of cartography did not come into vogue until the latter half of the 17th century. Before that time bird's eye views were drawn of cities. No scales could be attached to such perspective views, for buildings and streets which come in the foreground appear with greater prominence than buildings and streets in the far distance. Though it is not possible to apply a scale to these views, they do show the relative position of buildings as compared with their surroundings.

Fortunately for the purpose of identifying the position of the Globe Playhouse there is a long series of views of London taken from some imaginary point high above Southwark. The consequence is that the buildings of Southwark appear with great prominence, and the Globe Playhouse of Shakespeare stands out clearly. Before referring to these views in which the Globe appears it may be interesting to see one or two of Southwark as it was before the theatre was built. It is only possible to reproduce a small portion of these, as the original drawings are some feet in length. Hoefnagel's View of London 1572 (No. 1), a part of which is here reproduced, gives a picture of Southwark before the Globe was built. The main features to which attention should be drawn are the two circular buildings, situated above the heads of the two ladies in the foreground. The one on the left, or west side, is described as " The Bowll baytyng" and the one on the right, or east side, is called " The

Beare Bayting." They are prominent buildings in these views and they were the scenes of horrible and barbarous forms of amusement at that time. It will be shown ultimately that the Globe Playhouse occupies the exact site of the Bear baiting ring. If this point is established, it is well to note the position of the Bear baiting ring in its relation to its surroundings. To the east of the Bear baiting ring there is a well defined road running north and south. This road has two parallel lines drawn down its centre, and here and there are short parallel lines, crossing them.

The parallel lines running down the centre of the road show the open ditch or sewer, and the cross parallel lines are bridges over the sewer. This roadway, formerly known as Deadman's Place, is today known as Bank End. It will be seen that there is a short way or lane leading out of Deadman's Place which gives access to the Bear baiting ring as indicated by arrows in the margin of the view. There is a bridge over the sewer in Deadman's Place immediately opposite the way or lane, and on the eastern side of Deadman's Place there is a roadway shown almost in alignment with the way or lane. This roadway was then (as it is today) known as Clink Street.

The main point, however, of Hoefnagel's view lies in the fact that there are two parallel lines with a hedge on the northern side, at the southern end of the gardens of the Bull and the Bear baiting rings and the garden between them, which has three ponds shown upon it, and the little garden behind the house in Deadman's Place, see indicating arrows.

These parallel lines are intended to show a common sewer, and the direction that the sewer takes is the same that is taken by Maiden Lane afterwards.

This sewer therefore is in all probability the northern of the two sewers which Strype tells us existed in Maiden Lane. The great open space to the south of this sewer is the Lord Bishop of Winchester's Park.

Already, and pretty well a generation before the Globe was built, the early developments seem to be falling into line with what we are told in the Osteler document. If we assume, for the moment, that the Bear baiting ring ultimately became the site of the Globe, then we see the beginning of the way or lane which divided the two pieces of land granted by Brend to Burbage in 1599. We see again that the southern of the two pieces of land fronts upon the ditch or sewer where Maiden Lane was constructed afterwards.

This view of Hoefnagel's should now be compared with the view by Agas (No. 2) which is also reproduced. Agas's view is of just about the same date as Hoefnagel's, and the striking similarity between them shows that one copied the other.

Possibly Hoefnagel's is the earlier. The difference between the two views lies in the fact that in Hoefnagel's we see the sewer which afterwards was the northern sewer of Maiden Lane. In consequence the position of Maiden Lane is indicated in the view. We also see the great park of the Lord Bishop of Winchester.

Agas's view, on the other hand, does not show the northern sewer of Maiden Lane nor the Bishop's Park. They both lie too far south, and so they are outside the picture. There can be no doubt that the two prominent polygonal buildings shown by Agas are the same two buildings shown by Hoefnagel. The same way or lane is shown by both, leading out of Deadman's Place (see indicating arrows).

In examining the view of London by Norden (No. 3) which is inscribed " Pieter Vanden Keere fecit 1593," here reproduced, we see that certain changes in the development of Southwark have taken place since Hoefnagel prepared his view some twenty years before the Globe was built.

By comparing Norden's view with Hoefnagel's it will be seen that in Norden's Maiden Lane has been carried through to Deadman's Place and both its northern and southern sewers or ditches are shown, as indicated by arrows. The northern sewer shown by Norden is obviously the same as Hoefnagel shows. This sewer, in both views, forms the southern boundary of the gardens of the Bull and Bear baiting rings.

A few houses have been built on the eastern extension of Maiden Lane, they stand on what appeared to be the vacant land of the Lord Bishop of Winchester's Park in Hoefnagel's view. The point of interest in Norden's view lies in the fact that the Bear baiting ring, so clearly shown by Hoefnagel and Agas, has now disappeared. The bear baiting is now shown to be carried on in the old Bull baiting ring.

The disappearance of the old Bear baiting ring is important, as when this was pulled down, a vacant site was created. This vacant site in the midst of the pleasure resorts, on the south side of the river, would no doubt appeal to Richard and Cuthbert Burbage, Shakespeare and the other actors who were part proprietors in the Globe Playhouse yet to be built. The south side of the Thames was not, to the same degree, ruled by the Privy Council and the Puritanical City Fathers.

I have already stated, that it would be shown that the Globe Playhouse occupied the site of the Bear baiting ring as shown both by Hoefnagel and Agas. In support of this statement a portion of Visscher's view of London 1616, is reproduced (No. 4). If this is compared with Hoefnagel's and Agas's views, made some 50 years earlier, it is impossible to deny that "The Globe," standing in the centre of Visscher's view absolutely coincides with the site previously occupied by the "Beare bayting ring" in the earlier views. The way or lane leading out of Deadman's Place is again shown by Visscher and it now apparently gives access to the site of the theatre.

In Visscher's view the theatre is named, for the words "The Globe" appear immediately over the building to which they obviously refer.

It may here be remarked that the Globe Playhouse was built in 1599, and burnt down in 1613. It was immediately rebuilt, on the same site, and it was finally pulled down in 1644. This view of Visscher's was therefore made during the lifetime of the second Globe.

Unfortunately this view of Visscher's, like several others, stops short of showing Maiden Lane. Maiden Lane lies to the south of these views, therefore everything shown in the views must lie to the north of that lane.

This contemporary evidence is invaluable in locating the site of the Globe: but the evidence by no means rests only on Visscher's testimony.

Merian's view of London c. 1638 (No. 5),—Vanden Hoeye's view of about the same date,—the Profil de la ville de Londre by Boisseau—all show the Globe and name it.—Merian doing so by an index number, 37, and by reference to the index 37 is found to be the Globe.

There is, however, a great similarity amongst these views, all showing the distinct influence of Visscher, but, apart from these, the great map-maker, Hollar, made a drawing of London which was published in 1647 (No. 6), though it was probably prepared several years earlier, for he was in banishment from England between the years 1643 and 1652. He also shows the Globe and names it. Hollar's drawing is taken from a different bird's eye point of view; but the Globe appears in it just behind the cottages fronting upon Bankside, but in some respects there is considerable divergence of expression as to the surroundings of the theatre, as compared with Visscher's view.

Then there is F. de Wit's view of London (No. 7), here reproduced, in which the playhouse is again shown and named. There is one other view "Londinum urbs praecipua regni Angliae" (No. 8) which, I believe, has never been published. In it, the Globe is again shown, and referred to by an index number.

The main point in all these views, lies in the fact that in all cases the Globe is shown to be standing on the north side of Maiden Lane.

The view by Hondius (No. 11) of London 1610 shows a circular building in the foreground. This is sometimes regarded as the Globe, though there is nothing definite to guide us to this conclusion. This circular building is, in all probability, the Rose Playhouse built by Philip Henslowe.

If a comparison is made between the Hondius view and that of Norden in 1593 it will be seen that the two buildings with their flags flying above them in the Hondius view correspond fairly well in point of relative position with "The Playhowse" and "The Beare Howse" shown by

Norden. Therefore there is some probability that in each view the same two buildings are shown. If so then the circular building shown by Hondius cannot be the Globe, for the circular "Playhowse" which corresponds with it in Norden's view of 1593 was engraved some six or seven years before the Globe was built. That the Hondius view was on sale in 1610 and possibly published in that year does not preclude the possibility of it having been drawn some years earlier. But apart from this uncertainty there is nothing to show that this theatre stood on the south side of Maiden Lane.

We may now consider maps of London prepared long after the Globe was pulled down in 1644.

Morden and Lea's map of London c. 1682 (No. 9) or later, shows a remarkable development of Southwark towards the end of the 17th century. The Lord Bishop of Winchester's Park is covered by roads, gardens and houses, Maiden Lane now appears as "Made Lane" and lying to the south of it is a narrow passage way, which at its western end takes a right angle turn to the north into "Made Lane." This passage was called "Globe Alley." It is shown much more clearly in Rocque's Plan of London 1746 (No. 10). It is opposite the "a" in Dead of Deadman's Place. When it came into existence seems uncertain; but probably it was formed after the Globe Playhouse had been built, and it was probably named after this great outstanding building had been erected.

Mr Braines, the author of the London County Council pamphlet on "The Site of the Globe Playhouse, Southwark" points out that

an indenture of 13th January 1635–6 between Sir Matt. Brend and Wm. Smyter refers to premises which are abutting on Mayden Lane aforesaid towards the North and a certain lane now called Globe Alley towards the South, (Close Roll 3063) so that eight years before the Globe was pulled down (1644) a Globe Alley was in existence to the South of Maid Lane.

the date of this other document is 1626, and the question will arise then, as to whether the Globe Alley referred to in the 1635 document, quoted by Mr Braines, is the same Globe Alley that is referred to in the 1626 document, or whether it refers to another Globe Alley on the north side of Maiden Lane.

This 1626 document is one of very great interest and deals with the sale of most of the property lying on the north side of Maiden Lane.

Particulars are contained in P.R.O. (Close Rolls, 3 Chas. 1, Part 23, 22). It is referred to by Dr Martin in his pamphlet on the "Site of the Globe Playhouse" on p. 21, and it is also referred to in the London County Council official pamphlet by Mr Braines.

In both cases the reference is incomplete and important matter which has a distinct bearing on the site of the Playhouse is unfortunately omitted. Perhaps this omission may have led these researchers to their wrong conclusion. The Close Roll, however, falls into line with other contemporary documents, and it is the harmony that exists amongst the authorities which gives them the stamp of accuracy.

Incidentally the information it contains adds greatly to our knowledge of the locality, and, particularly so, by showing that the way or lane, opening out of Deadman's Place, opposite Clink Street, was in fact a north side "Globe Alley" which led to the Globe Playhouse. This is exactly what might be imagined after inspecting the map-views which show the way or lane leading to the Globe Playhouse; but the way or lane has not been named, so far as is known, in an earlier document. In this transfer, which we are about to consider, this way or lane is named and it is called "Globe Alley."

The Globe Alley on the south of Maiden Lane, obviously extremely narrow, could never, in the very nature of things, have been a suitable approach to the famous Globe Playhouse, even if the theatre had been on the south side of Maiden Lane. It is impossible to imagine that such an approach could have been in keeping with the words of Ben Jonson: "The Globe, the glory of the Bank."

Such a description would be appropriate to a building on the north side of Maiden Lane : but it could hardly apply to a site away south on the south side of Maiden Lane. The chief patrons would come from the north side of the Thames, and would land at the Stairs, at the north end of Deadman's Place. The theatre, if on the north side, would have been within a stone's throw, and the way or lane, leading to it, within a few yards of the Stairs.

Now as to this transfer which, in future, will be called the Hillarie Memprise document. It is an "Indenture made the 11th December, 2 Charles, between Sir Matthew Brend of West Moulsey, Co. Surrey, Knight, of the one part, and Hillarie Memprise, Citizen and Habberdasher of London of the other part."

Sir Matthew Brend "for the consideration of the sum of £633 of good and lawful money of England" sells the fee simple of a good deal of property. Much of this property was let for a considerable term of years, the leases having been granted by Sir John Bodley the uncle and guardian of Matthew Brend during his infancy. After Brend came of age he personally granted some of the leases mentioned in the deed.

Now all these properties are described in the transfer and then we get these words :

And all those messuages tenements houses, edifices buildings gardens orchards wharfes plotts void and wast ground and all other land and hereditaments whatsoever with all and singular their appertunances scituate lying and being in Mayden Lane in the parish of St. Saviour alias St. Mary Overies in Southwark in the County of Surrey.

Up to this point there is nothing to determine whether this property was on the north or south side of Maiden Lane, but the deed continues and soon settles that point :

which said messuages tenements houses edifices land gardens void and wast ground and other pmisses are bounded with the King's high-way called Deadman's Place on the east and upon the Brooke or common shewer dividing them from the Parke of the Lord Bishopp of Winchester on the South and the garden comonly called the lumbard garden on the west and the alley or way leading to the Gloabe Playhouse comonly called Gloabe Alley on the North.

It is quite obvious that if Globe Alley is the boundary on the north, and Deadman's Place is the boundary on the east and Lombard Garden is the boundary on the west, then this property which is described "scituate lying and being in Mayden Lane" must have been bounded by the sewer in Maiden Lane on the south; a sewer which in a general broad sense divided the land from the Lord Bishop of Winchester's Park. The property, or some of it, is stated to be in Maiden Lane, and this lane, or the northern sewer in it, was, just as surely, the southern boundary, as Globe Alley is stated to have been the boundary on the north.

There is no getting away from the text—Globe Alley leading to the Globe Playhouse was on the north of Maiden Lane. Therefore the Globe Alley which appears in Rocque's view on the south side of Maiden Lane was not the Globe Alley leading to the Globe Playhouse or the one referred to in this document. We fear that this south side Globe Alley has been accountable for misleading so great an authority as Rendle. And both Dr Martin and Mr Braines have assumed this south side Globe Alley to be the one referred to in the Hillarie-Memprise deed. Having established the fact that there was a Globe Alley on the north, we may proceed with the deed. Certain measurements are given to us, for the deed says the property comprising these various parcels of land

"Contaynes in length from the King's high way called 'Deadman's place' in the east to the aforesaid garden called the lumber or lumbard garden on the west 270 foote or thereabout" (not 317 as Dr Martin states) "and in breadth from the path called Gloabe Alley on the North to the Comon shewer on the South 124 foote or thereabout."

The position of the way or lane, just opposite Clink Street in Deadman's Place, now known to be Globe Alley, is clearly defined.

The distance from Globe Alley on the north to the common sewer on the south is stated to be 124 feet. With a tape I have measured that distance and I find that it exactly coincides with what must have been the northern of the two sewers in Maiden Lane. This is a valuable confirmation of the position of Globe Alley, and incidentally of the accuracy of the document.

Here it should be recalled that there were two pieces of land which were leased by Brend to the brothers Burbage, Shakespeare and others.

These two pieces of land were divided by a way or lane now known to be Globe Alley. The southern of these two pieces has been included in the sale from Sir Matthew Brend to Hillarie Memprise. The Globe Playhouse could not therefore have stood on the southern piece, so it must in consequence have stood on the northern piece. This is exactly what we should have imagined from the map-views.

Sir Matthew Brend, by this same document appears to have sold a portion of his land on the north side of Globe Alley.

The deed, after giving particulars of the property, describes it as

being in Mayden Lane aforesaid in the parish of St. Saviour...and bounded on the South with the said alley called Gloabe Alley and on the east with the aforesaid high way called Deadman's Place and upon the North upon the tenement and yard of Thomas Gunn, and Westwarde on the yarde of the tenement or house called the back part of a tenement called the 'Ship.'

This piece of land must have been quite small, for its northern boundary is only Thomas Gunn's tenement or yard, and its western boundary is only the yard of a tenement called the Ship.

Globe Alley is described as being the boundary on the north of the first lot of properties described, and it becomes the boundary on the south of the second lot, thus showing that some of the property lay on the north side and some on the south side of Globe Alley.

There is thus a striking similarity in the description given of the land mentioned in the Osteler transcript and that given in the Hillarie Memprise document. There can be no doubt that "the way or lane" mentioned in the former document is in fact the Globe Alley in the latter.

Those who claim that the theatre stood on the south side of Maiden Lane, must of necessity also transfer this land, mentioned in the Hillarie Memprise document, to the south side of Maiden Lane; otherwise the theatre would be standing on the south side of Maiden Lane and the Globe Alley, which led to it, would be left on the north side.

It was by assuming an error in the orientation of the Osteler document that Dr Martin and Mr Braines reached the conclusion that the Globe was on the south side of Maiden Lane and not on the north, and now in order to get the land mentioned in the Hillarie Memprise deed transferred to the south side of Maiden Lane, it will be necessary to contend that the orientation in this document is also at fault. For as the deed stands the land is bounded on the north by Globe Alley and on the south by Maiden Lane. To transfer the land to the other side of Maiden Lane it would have to be bounded on the south by Globe Alley and on the north by Maiden Lane. The wording of the transfer is perfectly clear and there should be no misjudging it. The vital words "scituate lying and being in Mayden Lane" if read in conjunction with the fact that the land was bounded on the north by Globe Alley, precludes the possibility that it could have been on the south side of Maiden Lane.

The various references to wharfs, in this Memprise document, suggest river-side frontages, or, perhaps properties near the river[1]. Many of the great ditches or sewers which discharged in the Thames, did have small wharves on their sides, but it does not seem likely that there would be wharves to an inland site, such as the south side of Maiden Lane, unless the word "wharf" had a different meaning in those days. The various extracts previously reported by Dr Martin and Mr Braines have not included these references to the wharves; and it seems to me that it has a suggestive bearing upon the subject[2].

It should always be remembered that contemporary evidence is the best evidence, and though the language then, as today, may be a little involved, the meaning and intention is generally perfectly clear. The documents should be taken at their face value, that is to say the meaning they are intended to convey should be accepted. It is necessary to make this fact perfectly clear, and it is repeated, perhaps more than enough, so that it should not be forgotten. Some researchers, on quite insufficient and indeed false

[1] See Note 3, p. 44.   [2] See Note 4, p. 44.

grounds, have construed the language of these deeds as conveying the precise opposite of that which they clearly state.

Dr William Martin, M.A., LL.D., F.S.A., in his pamphlet (reprinted from *Surrey Archaeological Collections*, Vol. XXIII. in 1910), gives us a good deal of very interesting information, and, moreover, the references are very ample: the pamphlet shows that there has been a good deal of research work done, which has contributed to making the task easier for those who follow him in writing on the subject. In support of the contention that the site of the Globe was on the south side of Maiden Lane he points out on p. 23 that amongst the deeds in the possession of Messrs Barclay Perkins & Co., who own the land on the south side of Park Street (Maiden Lane), is one dated 21st Dec. 1706 which is in effect a "Mortgage between Timothy Cason and Elizabeth, his wife of the one part and William James, Citizen and Merchant taylor of the other part." In this document these words occur:

All those messuages or tenements with their and every of their appurtenances situate and lying and being in or near Maiden Lane...most of which last before-mentioned messuages or tenements were erected and built where the late playhouse called the Globe stood and upon the ground thereunto belonging.

There is some reason to suppose that this document refers to some property mentioned in another document of 1726 also in the possession of Messrs Barclay Perkins & Co. This second document is between Timothy Cason and Elizabeth his wife of the first part and John Lade, James Kinder and other parishioners of the third part. Dr Martin points out that "Upon the plot, the subject of this document, a workhouse for the poor of Southwark was erected." It is assumed by the solicitors to Messrs Barclay Perkins & Co. that these two documents have relation to each other, and that they refer to the same plot of land. But, perhaps, this is not as clear as it might be, for the 1706 document refers to tenements and the 1726 document has reference to a workhouse. Still, it is quite possible that the tenements were pulled down and a workhouse was erected on the site, and so if it is granted that the two documents refer to the same plot of land there is the statement in the 1706 document that the tenements were erected "where the late playhouse called the Globe stood." Now having regard to the fact, that, as the workhouse site is on the south side of Maiden Lane these words do more than suggest that the theatre was also on the south side of Maiden Lane.

Tradition, however, is more often interesting than accurate. It must be remembered that the earlier document in question is dated sixty-two years after the theatre was pulled down. It must also be remembered that there was a Globe Alley on the south side of Maiden Lane, and in a span of sixty-two years, the life of two generations, it is very possible that the impression grew up that this southern Globe Alley was connected with the Globe Theatre. The original site of the theatre may well have been forgotten and it is not unreasonable to suppose that the tradition of the site would gravitate to somewhere in the neighbourhood of this southern Globe Alley.

It is well to put our trust in contemporary documents rather than in those of later date. It may be remembered that a piece of land called "The Park" was the northern boundary of the land leased by Brend to the brothers Burbage, Shakespeare and others, and that Maiden Lane formed the southern boundary.

On this point Dr Martin says:

But concerning the situation of the Park, presumably the park of the Bishop of Winchester, no evidence is yet forthcoming that the park ever lay to the North of Maid Lane, while there is ample evidence that it lay to the South and South-east of that thoroughfare (p. 16).

The Bishop's Park did at one time extend, on the north, right down to the river. This is apparent from Mackenzie Walcott's account of "William de Wyckham and his Colleges" (p. 85).

Winchester House in Southwark was built by William Giffard, Bishop of Winchester in 1106, on ground belonging to the Prior of Bermondsey, to whom he paid a yearly acknowledgement. It was a convenient residence for the prelate of that See when attending parliament.

On the south were a park and gardens, on the north flowed the Thames, under a noble terrace. On the East was the Priory and on the West, Paris gardens.

That the name "The Park" should have attached itself to some of this land, when the south side of the river was beginning to be developed seems not unnatural. To assume that the Park never existed on the north side of Maiden Lane, is now shown to be incorrect. The result, however, of this assumption is disastrous to Dr Martin's theory, for the whole position as described in the Osteler transcript becomes reversed. The Park which is described as being on the north now becomes, according to Dr Martin, on the south.

Dr Martin admits that

even though what is perhaps the more ready way of reading the extracts, is that which ought to be adopted, there is the possibility—one might say the probability—to be kept in mind of the draftsman of the document having been careless as regards the bearings of the area which he was describing (p. 18).

So Dr Martin would have us believe that the Osteler document should have described Maiden Lane as the northern boundary, and the park (presumed to be the Bishop of Winchester's park) should be the southern boundary. Thus, on his presumption of the error, the Globe Playhouse was on the south side of Maiden Lane, and not on the north as described in the document. Now let us consider this line of reasoning. First and foremost there is the presumption that the piece of land called "The Park" is the Lord Bishop of Winchester's park. This we know, from evidence already advanced, was not the case, and, moreover, when the Bishop's park was referred to in legal documents, it was the custom to call it "The Lord Bishop of Winchester's Park" and not simply "the Park." Throughout the evidence of the extracts quoted, this will be found to be the invariable custom. Legal documents, especially when dealing with sales or leases, do not generally err on the side of brevity. But, apart from this unfortunate assumption that the park was the Lord Bishop of Winchester's Park, there is another objection of a far more serious nature.

It must be remembered that the extract from the Osteler deed, describing the boundaries of the land, is a transcript from the original lease, which was granted by Nicholas Brend on 21st Feb. 1599, the term of the lease to begin from 25th Dec. 1598, the lessees being Cuthbert and Richard Burbage, William Shakespeare, Augustine Phillips, Thomas Pope, John Hemyngs and William Kemp, their Exors, administrators and assigns.

If there was a mistake in the transcript, in wrongly putting in the cardinal points, the same errors must have appeared in the original lease, of which it was a copy. The lessor, Nicholas Brend, was a large landed proprietor[1]—it is difficult to imagine that he should not have noticed the error. The lessees, Cuthbert and Richard Burbage, were business men, who had had much trouble with Giles Allen, their landlord of "The Theatre" at Shoreditch, and after their experience in connection with that lease, they are not likely to have overlooked the glaring error, in their new lease, for their next theatrical venture. Is it likely that Shakespeare was so careless, or so indifferent, as not to notice the mistakes? Phillips, Pope, Hemyngs and Kemp too were all directly interested in the great venture of the Globe Playhouse and they were the lessees of the Globe site. Is it possible that none of these men read through the lease? The assumption that none of these men detected the error is preposterous and unbelievable. And yet, it is only on this assumption, that the orientation is wrongly described in the lease, and again in the transcript, that it is possible to transfer the site of the Globe Playhouse from the north to the south side of Maiden Lane.

In the Osteler transcript there is no note or reference, to any sort of error, in the original lease, which might account for its repetition. Dr Martin furnishes a diagram in which everything is reversed from that which is stated in the Osteler indenture. He puts Maiden Lane to the north and the Park (in brackets " The Bishop of Winchester's ") to the south; this he considers " represents the state of affairs as thus derived, in the corrected manner set out, from the Osteler document." Dr Martin quotes from several 18th century documents which in all probability do refer to property on the south side of Maiden Lane. In the deed of 7th June, 1787, by which in effect Messrs Barclay & Perkins took over Thrale's Brewery, it appears

---

[1] See Notes 1 and 2, p. 44.

that "the before mentioned cellar fronting a certain Alley or passage called Globe Alley in ancient times leading from Deadman's Place aforesaid to the then Globe Playhouse" (pp. 25, 26), and again, Wadsworth to Ralph Thrale, 1732 messuages are conveyed "fronting a certain alley or passage called Globe Alley, in ancient times leading from Deadman's Place to the Globe Playhouse" (p. 26). These post-dated documents cannot override the contemporary documents. Their chief point of interest lies in the fact that in the course of a very few generations the actual site of the Globe Playhouse appears to have been forgotten. How many of us today would be able to identify a site of a demolished building, with nothing more to guide us than our childish recollections of what our grandfathers told us?

The 19th century sketch maps which Dr Martin reproduces show the Globe Theatre to the south of Maiden Lane; but again, their evidence has no weight as compared with the contemporary views. I am obliged to quote the following extract:

From a comparison of early London Maps, Mr George Hubbard F.S.A. in a well illustrated paper, thinks the site was adjacent to the present causeway by the river side, the modern Bankside. Neither the interpretation of the maps in his paper, however, nor the conclusions, drawn from them, are in accord with the present writer's views. Mr Hubbard's conclusions, moreover, are alone among those which are set out under the present heading (p. 35).

My views are by no means alone. They are held by Dr Wallace, and nobody can speak with greater authority on this particular point than he.

That great Shakespearian authority Mrs Stopes informs me that when she was hurrying out her "Burbage, and Shakespeare's Stage" to help the movement for the Actors' Memorial in St Leonards, Shoreditch, she had an accident which prevented her walking, so she accepted Dr Martin's reading as to the site of the Globe, until she was able to walk again. Then she went to read the Sewer Books, and was converted at once by them.

Joseph Quincy Adams in his map of London showing the Playhouses puts the Globe on the north side of Maiden Lane.

In reply to Dr Martin I can only state that I am reproducing the views in this work, and I believe that my interpretation of them is correct; but in any case the reader has the views before him and they speak for themselves. It is, however, with regret that I am compelled to point out that Dr Martin has misread the views. He has invariably mistaken " the way or lane " now known to be Globe Alley, for Maiden Lane. If a comparison is made between Hoefnagel's view and Visscher's it is perfectly clear that the line of the northern sewer in Maiden Lane in Hoefnagel's view lies to the south of the way or lane (Globe Alley) in Visscher's view. In the Visscher panorama of 1616 the three little cottages are fronting upon Globe Alley and not Maiden Lane as Dr Martin assumes.

Hoefnagel shows, by putting in the northern sewer, the direction taken later of Maiden Lane; but Visscher does not do so, as Maiden Lane lies outside his picture.

Dr Martin asserts:

As a result of the collation, it will be found that, with one notable exception, a playhouse either is shewn to the South of Maid Lane, or otherwise no positive information as to the playhouse relatively to Maid Lane is obtainable (p. 37).

Such a statement is not, I am afraid, borne out by the facts. I have before me, at the moment of writing, reproductions of seven contemporary views in all of which the Globe is shown and named, or marked with an index number. In each of these seven cases the Globe is shown to be on the north side of Maiden Lane. In some cases Maiden Lane lies too far south to appear in the view, as in Visscher's view; but as I have previously referred to these views it is unnecessary to do so again.

The notable exception to which Dr Martin refers as showing the Globe on the north side of Maiden Lane is in Visscher's view. Visscher shows the Globe on the north side of Maiden Lane and inscribes the name over it.

To get over the evidence of Visscher, Dr Martin adopts a highly ingenious and original suggestion. He says:

It is far from clear, however, that the polygonal building thus styled, which was evidently some sort of playhouse, or amphitheatre was in fact the Globe (p. 41).

I do not see what more the cartographer could have done than name the building he had drawn.

Owing to the unfortunate mistake of assuming that the way or lane shown in Visscher's view was Maiden Lane, Dr Martin is a little puzzled to account for the absence of another theatre, "The Rose," in Visscher's view, as this playhouse was on the north side of Maiden Lane.

Though the Rose was on the north side it still lay considerably to the south of the Globe and in consequence is outside Visscher's picture. Furthermore the life of the Rose was from 1587–1605, according to Joseph Quincy Adams. As Visscher's view was published in 1616, the Rose had disappeared some 10 or 11 years earlier.

Dr Martin continues by saying:

in Visscher there is no trace of the Rose, while the Globe is placed where the Rose would be expected (p. 41).

It would not be expected if Dr Martin had realised that the Rose had vanished years before the Visscher view was published or even if he had correctly read the view itself. "Therefore" he continues

Visscher or the Surveyor of the Panorama, having before him in the formation of his view the Braun map, and lacking intimate local information concerning what was then the relatively unimportant and possibly decaying Rose, but knowing by repute the renowned Globe, placed his Globe in the position of the Bear-pit of Braun, and omitted the Rose. To account correctly for the absence of the Rose and the placing of the building styled 'The Globe' on its site is not easy. It may well be that the Visscher Panorama, as originally drafted, contained the Globe in a position to the south of Maid Lane, and on curtailing the depth of the view for publication, or for some other purpose, the Globe was consequently removed from the picture, along with associated matter on either side, the style 'The Globe' within the limits of the picture being still allowed to remain. That the Panorama has been curtailed may be seen from the way in which its lower boundary sharply cuts through the line of hedging of Maid Lane (pp. 41 and 42).

It is not Maiden Lane, it is Globe Alley, that forms the southern boundary of the view.

Dr Martin further suggests that the Globe may have existed in Visscher's view, before it was cut down, and, that it was to the south side of Maiden Lane; but the style "The Globe" was allowed to remain in the picture. There is no justification for such an assumption, especially as other contemporary evidence is opposed to it. Why should Dr Martin assume that Visscher or the Surveyor of the panorama lacked intimate local information and so placed the Globe in the position of the bear pit? Dr Martin has, in the first instance, by a topsy-turvy argument reversed the evidence of the Osteler document, and now it becomes necessary to bring the Visscher view into line, and this he does by telling us that the "Surveyor of the panorama lacked intimate local information" or "that the Engraver mistook his instructions when preparing the plate" (p. 42).

As previously pointed out the evidence that the Globe was on the north side of Maiden Lane does not rest solely on Visscher's view—Merian, Vanden Hoeye, Boisseau, Hollar and De Wit all clearly indicate the same fact and name the theatre. In spite of this Dr Martin speaks of the Visscher view as being the only notable exception in placing the Globe to the north of Maiden Lane, but he finds the Merian view is also opposed to his theory. A reference to the Merian view shows that the two polygonal buildings, the Bear-pit on the west, and the Globe on the east, stand in their accustomed relative positions. The numbers 37 and 38 are found in the index to be the Bear Garden and the Globe. This is exactly in accordance with the evidence of other views; but Dr Martin, in order to bring the Merian view into line with his theory, informs us that this contemporary evidence is wrong.

"The Globe (37)" he says "should have been styled in the index as (The Rose) while the building (38)...is clearly the Globe. The Rose however is styled the Globe in the key at the base of Merian's Map, while the Globe is called the 'Bear Garden.'"

Dr Martin then continues to tell us

That the names have been wrongly marked, and that Maid Lane has been placed at an angle need not disturb us when we think of the convention and freedom adopted and exercised by engravers and artists in delineating the London of their days. From this map-view of Merian, then, we see the Globe assigned to a position south of Maid Lane (p. 44).

Again, there has been the same unfortunate error of mistaking the "Way or Lane" (Globe Alley) for Maiden Lane, and moreover we cannot "see the Globe assigned to a position south of Maid Lane," for the simple reason that Maiden Lane lies outside the view. Again there is the presumption of attempting to correct the contemporary evidence; and again there is the evidence that Dr Martin has not rightly understood the views.

In these circumstances it is not surprising that the conclusions he draws are open to very serious doubts and objections. With regard to Hollar's view he says:

'The Globe' appears prominently on the Surrey bank of the river. This building is shewn at the edge of the water (p. 45).

If the reader will refer to Hollar's view he will see that the Globe stands behind a row of cottages on Bankside, and not at the edge of the water. Dr Martin considers further that

the draftsman had no local knowledge. It would seem that he filled up the unplotted area from memory which was faulty (p. 45).

To sum up Dr Martin tells us that

Visscher's panorama...undoubtedly places the playhouse which it styles 'The Globe' on the north side of Maid Lane, but...for reasons set out, this attribution must be viewed with suspicion. The other maps of the series show, or are in favour of, a position south of the Lane; alternatively, their representations are such that no definite pronouncement is obtainable from them (pp. 49, 50).

I am entirely at variance with Dr Martin in this summing up, for the reasons which I hope I have made abundantly clear. I should, however, like to be permitted to point out that it is not wise to jump to conclusions that the contemporary evidence is wrong. It may not be perhaps always understood, but it must be conceded, that those who drew up the contemporary legal document and contemporary map views, are more likely to be right, in what they wrote, and what they drew, than is possible even to the ablest researcher, groping for information after the lapse of some three hundred years.

My reason for having dealt at such length with Dr Martin's views, lies in the fact that in October 1909 Sir Herbert Beerbohm Tree, the president of the Shakespeare Reading Society, unveiled a bronze pictorial memorial to commemorate Shakespeare's Playhouse "The Globe." The bronze was fixed upon the wall of the brewery of Messrs Barclay Perkins & Co. Ltd., the wall being situated upon the south side of Park Street, Maiden Lane.

In the memorial, there is a pictorial panel which is intended to represent that portion of Southwark where the Globe was erected. On this panel Dr Martin's name appears, so presumably he is responsible for its composition. It may be remembered that in his explanation as to the reason of the name "The Globe" appearing in Visscher's view, when the building to which it referred was absent, was due "to the curtailing or cutting down of the panorama." So Dr Martin in this pictorial panel has placed the Globe where he thinks it ought to be, i.e. on the south side of Maiden Lane. Under the bust of Shakespeare, which forms a very striking and beautifully executed part of the memorial, are the words "Here stood the Globe Playhouse of Shakespeare." Now if the contemporary evidence may be relied upon, the Globe did not stand anywhere near the memorial. Doubtless this memorial will last for centuries, and if nobody ever raises a protest, it may, in time, become accepted that the Globe did stand there. Having traversed Dr Martin's objections, I now turn to the London County Council official pamphlet prepared by Mr Braines.

In this official report of the London County Council on "The Site of the Globe Playhouse" it is surprising to find that, the whole evidence of the map-views is summarily dismissed in a footnote on p. 7. Mr Braines says "In view of the unreliability, in matters of detail, of the early map views of London, the evidence of both sides is limited to that of a documentary character." Thus in this brief footnote the whole of the valuable evidence of the long series of contemporary drawings, in which the Globe is either named or indexed, is swept aside. Whatever inaccuracies may, or may not, exist in matters of detail, there is the conclusive and unanimous opinion amongst those who saw the theatre, and named or numbered it, that it stood on the north side of Maiden Lane. Having thus disposed of the views, and if the research is now to be confined to the documentary evidence alone, it is interesting to see the methods adopted by Mr Braines for disposing of them also. It may be remembered that on 5th December, 1595, the jurors presented

John Wardner, William Sellers and all the landholders or their tenants that holde anie landes, gardeins, ground or tenements abutting upon the common sewer leading from Sellors gardein to the beare gardein to cast, cleanse & scowre etc.

Also on the 14th February, 1605–6, the Commissioners made the following order:

It is ordered that Burbage and Heminges and others the owners of the Play-house called the Globe in Maid Lane shall...pull up and take cleanse out the sewer the props or posts which stand under theire bridge on the North side of Mayd Lane.

"These items," Mr Braines says, "taken by themselves are insufficient to prove that the Globe was on the North side of Maid Lane." He admits also that these

"two entries are strongly confirmatory of the evidence already afforded by the lease transcript" (the Osteler document) "and the three taken together constitute a strong body of evidence in favour of a northern site" (p. 9).

I entirely agree, and I should feel inclined to add that these three documents, in the absence of any documentary evidence to the contrary, constitute definite proof that the Globe was on the north side of Maiden Lane. As we shall show directly, Mr Braines, having committed himself to the topsy-turvy argument in respect to the Osteler document, finds himself confronted with a difficulty in respect to William Sellers. The William Sellers mentioned in the Minutes of the Sewers Commission as being on the north side of Maid Lane, is, he admits, the same William

Sellers mentioned in the Osteler document. But as the Osteler document is wrong in describing the theatre to be on the north side of Maiden Lane, when it should have been on the south, some method has to be devised whereby Sellers should be also carried onto the south side of the road ; for, obviously, Sellers who occupied the site adjoining the Globe, cannot be left on the north side of the road when the theatre he adjoined was transplanted to the south side of the road.

Most researchers would have felt themselves confronted with an insuperable difficulty. Mr Braines, however, meets the case by the happy suggestion that " Sellers may quite conceivably have had two gardens one on each side of the road" (p. 9). Of course this is quite conceivable ; but unfortunately there is not the slightest evidence that he had another garden on the other side of the road.

Now we may pass on to the second order of the Commissioners where Burbage and Hemyngs are requested to carry out certain work to their bridge on the *north* side of Maiden Lane.

We should have thought, from this entry, that it was obvious that the theatre was on the north side of the Lane ; but to Mr Braines it is only suggestive that it was so. He says:

The fact that the owners of The Globe had a bridge over the sewer on the north side of Maiden Lane certainly suggests that the theatre was on that side, but it does not actually prove so much (p. 9).

I am sorry that Mr Braines leaves the matter in this somewhat inconclusive way. He gave us food for reflection in the case of Sellers, but he leaves us at a loose end with regard to this bridge over the sewer on the north side of the road, which belonged to Burbage, Hemyngs and the other owners of the Globe Playhouse.

These three contemporary documents all show that the Globe was on the north side of Maiden Lane, and no valid objection to their acceptance has yet been advanced, either by Dr Martin or Mr Braines.

Now we come to the Park which formed the northern boundary of the land mentioned in the Osteler deed. Here again it is necessary to quote at some length from Mr Braines's pamphlet.

The mention of 'the park,' however, in the lease transcript as the northern boundary of the site, constitutes a serious difficulty. The only 'Park' in the neighbourhood, it is said, was the well known park of the Bishop of Winchester which certainly lay to the *South* of Maid Lane, and it has been suggested that by some means the boundaries were reversed in the lease, and the actual position of the site was between Maid Lane on the North and the Park on the South (pp. 9 and 10).

It now appears because somebody has " *said* " that the only park in the neighbourhood was the well known park of the Bishop of Winchester, which certainly lay to the south of Maiden Lane, and because it has been " *suggested* " that the boundaries are reversed in the Osteler deed the direct evidence to the contrary of the contemporary documents is to count for nothing. It must not be forgotten that William de Wyckham informs us that the park extended up to the Thames where there was the noble terrace. Mr Braines has informed us that " the evidence on both sides was to be limited to that of a documentary character." I ask for nothing more; but when Mr Braines acts on a suggestion that by some means the boundaries were reversed in the lease and that Sellers might have had another garden on the other side of the road, and that the entry in the minutes of the Sewers Commission, when the lessees of the Globe were called upon to remove their props under their bridge on the north side of the road, does not prove that the Globe was on the north side, then I can only ask what weight does Mr Braines attach to the documents or what better or more conclusive evidence could he expect? But, to return to the Park—he asks the question " Is there any corroborative evidence for the existence of a Park on the North side of Maid Lane?" He answers the question by saying " Two such items of evidence have been brought forward (*a*) by Mr Geo. Hubbard (*b*) by Dr Wallace."

The evidence (*a*) I brought forward is contained in my paper read to the London and Middlesex Archaeological Society, 26th Feb. 1912. Mr Braines reviews this evidence and that of Dr Wallace—he says :

(*a*) Mr Geo. Hubbard states:

"that the position of the heading 'ffrom the park' in certain of the Sacramental Token Books proves that a property called 'The Park' was on Bankside. After pointing out that the token distributor in 1598 started from The Bell on Bankside, then next in topographical order the tokens were collected from the Clinck also on Bankside, then 'Widdowe Newton's Rents' after this comes the 'Stewes Rents.' These houses of ill fame were well known to be situated on Bankside. Unfortunately for Mr Hubbard's argument, it is not 'Stewes Rents' but 'Drewes Rents.' After 'The Stewes' (*sic*) we get Mr Newton's Rents and now we get to some property *while we are still on Bankside* which was then called 'The Park' for the entry in the Token Book stands as follows: 'ffrom the Park.'"

Mr Braines's comment on this is that

It will be observed that Mr Hubbard's only authority for the words in italics is his misreading of the entry 'Drewes Rents' (p. 10).

I should like to point out to Mr Braines that I made no mistake, the words *are* "Stewes Rents" and it occurs in the order as stated by me, "Drewes Rents" come in the list after "Hether Bank End." Perhaps Mr Braines will kindly correct this misstatement of fact if a further edition of his pamphlet is brought out by the London County Council. Also perhaps Mr Braines will kindly correct another misstatement. I did not speak of a "distributor" of tokens but a "collector" of tokens.

Dr Wallace, who has done more than anyone else in his discovery of documents to settle this question, is summarily dealt with.

It is not easy to follow Mr Braines's reasoning and therefore to avoid any chance of misrepresentation I quote him at length.

(*b*) Dr Wallace states that

"in dealing with the property of Brend and his tenants on the north side of Maiden Lane, the sewer Commission made the following entries...on 6th July 1593:

We present Jasper Morris of London, dyer, to pull up his encroachment made att the backe of his garden into the sewar betweene his garden and the parck....We present Thomas Burt, dyer, to pull upp his encrochmt. made upon the sewer running betwene the back of his garden and the parck...."

It will be remembered that Isbrand Morris and Thomas Burt were previous tenants of portions of the Globe site. If therefore, Dr Wallace's statement that these men were presented in the course of dealing with the *North* side of Maid Lane be true, the evidence is conclusive, that not only the gardens in question were on the North side, but that 'the parck' twice mentioned was also on that side. *The statement however is entirely without justification.* An examination of the entries and their context shows that there is no suggestion whatever that the properties dealt with were on one side of the road or the other. Both attempts to produce corroborative evidence as to the existence of a 'Park' to the North of Maid Lane therefore fail (pp. 11 and 12).

It would be interesting to hear what Dr Wallace might say in reply. It seems to me that his position is unassailable. The Osteler document tells us that Jasper Morris and Thomas Burt were tenants on the Brend Estate and they occupied a portion of the northern of the two pieces of land granted in the lease to Burbage brothers and others.

Dr Wallace is entirely guided by what the Osteler document says, when he quite logically assumed that the park in question was on the north side of Maiden Lane; and it is only by adopting the topsy-turvy argument, introduced by Dr Martin, which reverses the points of the compass, that could have inspired Mr Braines's remark "*That the statement however is entirely without justification.*" No valid argument has yet been advanced for the reversal of the cardinal points; and until this has been done, it should have been Mr Braines's plain duty to accept the clear statements of the Osteler and other documents.

If Mr Braines had checked my quotation from the Sacramental Token Books in Southwark Cathedral he might not have discarded, so lightly, the evidence I advanced that there was some property called "The Park" on Bankside.

Mr Braines does not consider the Minutes of the Surrey and Kent Commission as conclusive, on the question of the Park as distinct from the Bishop's Park.

There are some entries in these Minutes, he tells us, in which the Park is mentioned as meaning the Bishop's Park, and, *if* this is the case, he considers the words "The Park" must always mean the Bishop's Park. We cannot agree with this view, even if it is admitted that the words "The

Park" may sometimes mean the Bishop's Park, for it must be remembered that Minutes of the Surrey and Kent Sewers Commission are not legal engrossed documents, and the clerk who kept the Minutes would, after the name of the owner or occupier of the property had been entered, use the words "The Park" as sometimes meaning the Bishop's Park and sometimes the Park on the north side of Maiden Lane. The notice would be served upon the owner or occupier, and there could be no possible confusion, for the owner would know perfectly well which park was adjoining his property.

Mr Braines, perhaps not quite logically, attempts to put the onus of proof that the Globe was on the north side of Maiden Lane on those who hold that view. For he tells us that

on the assumption that the theatre was on the North side of the road...the following facts will have to be taken into account:

    1. The frontage of the Globe site was according to the lease transcript 156 feet.

    2. The site lay somewhere to the East of Rose Alley.

    3. The site was on the freehold of the Brend family, during the whole of the 17th Century (p. 14).

To make the matter clear Mr Braines has prepared a plan here reproduced by kind permission of the London County Council. Then, after

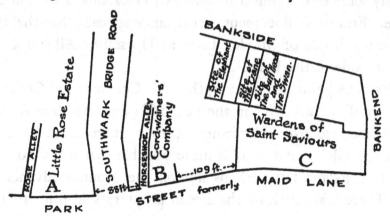

PLAN B.

laying down these "facts" (?) which have to be taken into account, Mr Braines proceeds to tell us that a property

(A) known as the 'Little Rose Theatre' was granted in the middle of the 16th Century by Tomasyn Symonds to the parish of St Mildred, Bread Street. It still belongs to the parish and so no part could have formed part of the Brend property in the 17th Cent. (pp. 14, 15).

I do not for a moment suggest that the Globe stood on this land, so we can pass on to the property marked (B).

During the 17th Century the Cordwainers' Company, by request and purchase, came into possession of a considerable estate in the neighbourhood of Horse Shoe Alley. On 21st October 1681 the Company leased to Christopher Marshall[1] *inter alia* a parcel of enclosed ground 'whereupon the Salt Peter house sometime before stood, containing in length by ye way leading through Horshoe Yard into ye Playhouse called ye Globe (to) the Ditch or comon shore on ye south parte, eighty one foot...and in breadth at ye south end thereof by the common shower next ye Lane there called Maid Lane on the South parte to ye comon shower on the east part fifty nine foot' &c. The frontage therefore for a distance of 59 feet eastward from Horseshoe Alley was in 1681 in the possession of the Cordwainer's Company, and no part of it can have formed a portion of the Globe Estate (p. 15).

Here there is much to be considered. Horseshoe Alley runs between Maiden Lane on the south and Bankside on the north (vide Rocque's plan, where Horseshoe Alley appears in the N.W. corner of the map). There is obviously some close connection between Horseshoe Yard and the Globe Playhouse. From this document it certainly appears that the Playhouse was on the north side of Maiden Lane as Horseshoe Alley does not exist on the south side of the Lane.

Mr Braines's point is, however, that the Cordwainers' Company were in possession of the site "B" in the year 1681 and therefore for a distance of 59 feet eastward from Horseshoe Alley no part could have formed a portion of the Globe estate. It is quite possible that it did not form part of the Globe Estate, but perhaps not on the grounds advanced by Mr Braines. There was much of the Brend property sold prior to 1681. So if the Cordwainers owned the property with a frontage to Maiden Lane of 59 feet in 1681, it is no evidence, in itself, that it could not have been, at

[1] *Chancery Proceedings*, Bridges, B. 333/2.

some earlier date, included in the Brend estate. We do not, however, suggest that the theatre did stand on this site having a frontage of 59 feet, so there is no need to go further into the matter.

With regard to "C" Mr Braines points out

"that the Churchwardens of St Saviour's were constituted a body corporate to whom was granted the property belonging to the Fraternity of the Assumption of our Lady" (p. 15). This property "consisted chiefly of an estate situated at the east end of the northern frontage of Maid Lane."

This property has a frontage of 247 feet to Park Street (Maiden Lane). It was in 1689, and still is, in the hands of the Wardens of St Saviour's.

That the property was in the hands of the Wardens of St Saviour's as early as 1689 does not show that it could not have been in the Brend Estate at an earlier date. I hope to show that this particular property with its frontage of 247 feet was in fact a part of the land sold by Brend to Memprise. It would be interesting to discover, if such information is available, whether the Wardens acquired the land from Memprise or from some other intermediate owner.

For the moment I will deal with the facts (?) which Mr Braines tells us have to be taken into account.

1. "The frontage of the Globe site was, according to the lease transcript (Osteler document) 156 feet."

I agree so far as the southern of the two pieces of land is concerned; but I do not believe that the Playhouse was built on that site. It stood I believe on the northern of the two pieces of land leased to Burbage, Shakespeare and others.

2. "The site lay somewhere to the East of Rose Alley."

I quite agree in this.

3. "The site was the freehold of the Brend family during the whole of the 17th century."

This I deny.

I have dealt at considerable length with the sale of land from Brend to Memprise in the year 1626 which clearly shows that the site was *not* the freehold of the Brend family during the whole of the 17th century. I will now attempt to show that this Brend to Memprise sale included the land acquired by the Church Wardens of St Saviour's, which has a frontage of 247 feet to Park Street (Maiden Lane).

If this can be satisfactorily shown it supplies the answer to Mr Braines's statement that the property marked C "could not have been a part of the Brend Estate in the 17th Cent."

Now as to the facts.

Mr Braines tells us that the Wardens Estate extended to Bank End (Deadman's Place). If Deadman's Place was the eastern boundary and it had a frontage of 247 feet on Maiden Lane, it must have formed a part and parcel of the land sold by Brend to Memprise which was bounded also on the east by Deadman's Place and had a frontage of 270 feet to Maiden Lane.

Therefore this particular site, now in possession of the Wardens of St Saviour's, was originally a part of the Brend Estate. If this is correct then Mr Braines is wrong in stating that this property "could not have been a part of the Brend estate in the 17th century." He does not show that the Wardens of St Saviour's have any older title to the land than from 1689, whereas Brend sold this same land to Memprise in 1626.

After showing to his satisfaction that the site of the Globe could not have been on either A, B or C he is forced to the conclusion that "*The Globe could not have been on the North side of Maid Lane!*" (p. 17).

Mr Braines need not have despaired, for it will be remembered that in the lease granted by Nicholas Brend to the brothers Burbage, Shakespeare and others there were two parcels of land. When Brend sold land to Hillarie Memprise it had a frontage of 270 feet to Maiden Lane, this in all probability absorbed the southern parcel of land granted in the lease to Burbage and others. The northern piece of land still remained in the hands of Burbage and others, and it was on this piece of land that the Globe stood.

This fact is clearly shown in the map views which unfortunately carry no weight with Mr Braines.

It is perhaps unnecessary to continue to follow Mr Braines's argument by which he attempted to show that the Globe must have stood on the south side of Maiden Lane. It seems that both he and Dr Martin decline to recognise that any land on the north side of Maiden Lane was known as the Park. The only Park they recognise is the Lord Bishop of Winchester's Park on the south side of Maiden Lane, and so we must agree to differ.

That the name "The Park" should have attached itself to some of this land, when the south side of the river was beginning to be developed, seems not unnatural.

That there was a piece of land which kept the name of the "Park" on the north side of Maiden Lane is clearly shown by the several references in the various deeds which have been quoted.

The pronouncement by the London County Council has a certain weight, simply from its official character, and possibly that body may be contemplating some other way of officially marking the site. It is to be hoped, before they take such a step, that the evidence I have tried to establish may be considered by them.

There is one further piece of evidence, which, though it carries weight with me, cannot equally appeal to others. This evidence I quote from my paper read before the London and Middlesex Archaeological Society.

In 1907 some foundations were being put in for a large warehouse now known as 6 and 7 Bankside. At the time the excavations were made I was not especially interested in the site of the theatre, and old foundations were thoughtlessly excavated and removed where they interfered with the proposed new works.

As a result no careful plan was made but such evidence as I have since been able to obtain convince me, beyond all doubt, that they were the actual foundations of the famous playhouse. Fortunately the Clerk of Works, who was engaged upon the new building, has been able to supply me with some information....In a letter he tells me that one of the foundations was approximately 20 feet in length and that it was about three feet thick. It was built upon planks supported on wooden piles. This foundation was under the southern wall of the new warehouses, and the wall was approximately parallel with the river Thames. The old foundation was reduced in width to about two feet at a depth of six feet below the ground line.

Another wall he describes, "as about ten feet long and three feet wide, it rested on planks and piles and the top of the wall was about four feet below the ground line."

The bricks used in these walls were the small common kind used in buildings of the Elizabethan period. But apart from these old foundations, I am in a position to give some account of the buildings which stood on the site before the warehouses were erected.

In 1907 an old dwelling house which was then occupied by a bottle merchant, stood on the site of 6 and 7 Bankside. The house was erected about the year 1750 and the old Elizabethan foundations had no relation whatever to this dwelling house. We know that when Sir Matthew Brend pulled down the Globe Playhouse in 1644 he erected tenements on the site. The reasonable life of such tenements would be about 100 years. If they were built in 1644–5 and their life is taken at 100 years they would be pulled down about 1750 or just about the date when the house, occupied later by the bottle merchant, was erected.

Now the Elizabethan foundations standing on wooden piles and elm boards, were as unsuitable to the tenements as they were to the dwelling house.

The question now arises, if these Elizabethan foundations had no connection either with the tenements or the dwelling house, then what building, of an Elizabethan period, requiring such massive foundations could have stood on this site?

If we turn to Agas's view and look at the "Beare Bayting" ring we realize that this wooden structure, could not have required the solid foundations exposed in 1907; but the second Globe Playhouse, built in 1613–14 and standing exactly on the site of the bear ring would have done so.

It is impossible to scale distances from these early map views; all that can be done, in the absence of definite measurements stated in the deeds, is roughly to determine the relative positions of buildings.

From Visscher's view we see that the Globe stood on the north side of Globe Alley which is immediately opposite Clink Street in Bank End (Deadman's Place). The distance between Globe Alley and the northern sewer in Maiden Lane (Park Street) is given to us as 124 feet in the Memprise document and the distance of Globe Alley on the south to Bankside on the north would be about 100 feet. This distance of 100 feet would be sufficient to allow for the depth of the cottages possibly known as the Park on Bankside, the width of Globe Alley and still leave sufficient space for the Playhouse.

The position of the Globe can only be judged from the map views, and, so far as they represent its relative position, it appears to be as nearly as possible coincident with 6 and 7 Bankside, where the Elizabethan foundations were discovered.

Whether these Elizabethan foundations are in fact the actual foundations of the second Globe, cannot probably be definitely determined. There is nothing inherently impossible in this, for, both from the point of view of date, and position, there is much to support the suggestion.

When the foundations at 6 and 7 Bankside were being excavated, certain old bits of pottery, some curious glazed tiles with an embossed pattern upon them, a few pipes and various odds and ends were discovered. They were collected together as they were found and they are now contained in a glass case in the new buildings. They were discovered within the contained area of the old foundations and therefore they may quite conceivably be directly connected with the Second Globe Theatre. These objects are here shown from a photograph which was taken of them before the glass case was made to receive them.

There is one other point which is worth recording, and that is in connection with Globe Alley on the north side of Maiden Lane. The back of the premises 6 and 7 Bankside are opposite some premises held under lease by Messrs Barclay Perkins & Co., the freeholders being the Wardens of St Saviour's, Southwark. The warehouses 6 and 7 Bankside have their frontage upon Bankside and the frontage of the premises belonging to the Wardens is upon Park Street (Maiden Lane). There is an open space between the backs of these two premises some ten feet wide.

Neither the Wardens, nor the freeholders of 6 and 7 Bankside have any title to this open space. It is a sort of no man's land, and my recollection of it is that it formed a part of a passage way between the backs of the warehouses fronting upon Bankside, and the backs of the warehouses fronting upon Park Street. Now however encroachments have been made upon it and it is not nearly so traceable as it used to be, five and twenty years ago. The position of this passage way corresponds with the position of the north side of Globe Alley, and though little remains of it today, it was originally, I am convinced, the Globe Alley which led to the Globe Playhouse of Shakespeare. My conviction was announced on the upper frontage of 6 and 7 Bankside, before the Park Street Bronze Memorial was affixed. The inscription can be read from the river and its northern Bank, and from Southwark Bridge on the West, to the South-Eastern and Chatham Railway Bridge on the East:

HERE STOOD THE GLOBE PLAYHOUSE OF SHAKESPEARE.
1599—1644

TERMINAL NOTES.

A few further points may be noted :

1. The ground in question was bought by Thomas Brend, Skrivenor, from John Young (Close Rolls, 1 and 2, P. and M. 504).

2. The Inquis. Post Mortem of Thomas Brend was held on 16 May 1599. It seems to refer to the Theatre. (See Inq. P. M. 2nd Series Chancery 257, 68.)

3. In the Sessions Court of the Sewers Commission 11 Eliz. (1569) p. 4ᵇ, is entered: "Wee present Thomas Brend of the Cittie of London Skrivenor." Threatening a fine if he did not cleanse his sewers. In 1585 "Thomas Brend and his tenants to cleanse the sewers." In 1587 "Thomas Brend and his tenant to pyle, boorde, wharfe and fill up with earth his Wharfe in Maiden Lane."

4. The special proof given by the sessions presenting the owners of the Playhouse for the encroachments under the Bridge over "their Sewers to the north of Maiden Lane" has been given, but no one has concluded the entry.

"Burbidge. It is ordered that the said Burbidge, Hemynges and others as aforesayd shall, before the 20th daie of Aprill next, well and sufficiently pyle, boorde, and fill up 8 poles more or lesse of their *Wharfe* against the said Playhouse upon payne and forfeit for every pole then undone 20/- (not done *decret novi levandum*)."

5. In the Contract for building the Fortune in Cripplegate, it is stipulated that it should be after the pattern of "the late erected Playhouse ON THE BANK in the Parish of St Saviours called the Globe." 1599.

INDEX

Plate 1

Sewer North of ↓ Maiden Lane

Way or ↓ Lane

Sewer North of ↓ Maiden Lane

Hoefnagel's View of London, 1572

Plate 2

Way or Lane

Way or Lane

re Crans

The Banck

The Beare bayting

The bolſe bayting

Agas' View of London, circa 1560-70 or later.

Norden's Map of London 1593.

Maiden Lane carried through to Dead Man's Place

Plate 4

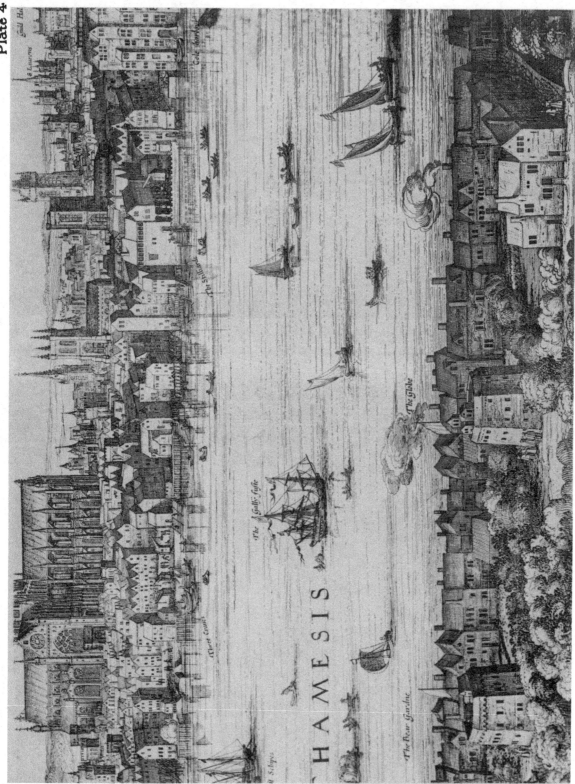

Visscher's View of London 1616.

Plate 5

Merian's View of London circa 1640-1638?

Plate 6

Hollar's View of London, 1647.

Plate 7.

F. de Wit's *View of London.*

Londinum Urbs praecipua regni Angliæ
See Merian 1638.

Globe Alley ⍒ South of Maiden Lane

Morden and Lea's Map of London circa 1682 probably later.
from London Topog. Soc's reproduction.

Plate 10

Globe Alley↓South of Maiden Lane

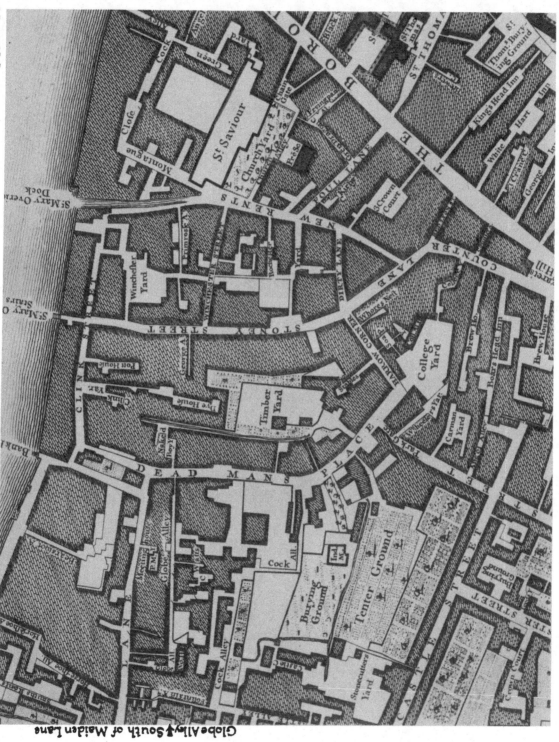

Rocque's Plan of London 1754.

Globe Alley↓South of Maiden Lane

Plate 11.

It was a circular wooden building, the centre being open to the sky, but the stage and galleries protected from the weather by thatch. The only authentic representation of this old theatre which I have yet met with is in the foreground of an interesting view of London in the corner of a map of Great Britain

Hondius' View of London, 1610, *from* Speed's "Theatre of the Empire of Great Britain."

and Ireland, "graven by I. Hondius and are to be solde by I. Sudbury and George Humble in Popes head Alley in London, 1610," and inserted in Speed's Theatre of the Empire of Great Britaine, 1611. The fac-simile of this view here given is carefully taken from a copy of the original edition of 1610.

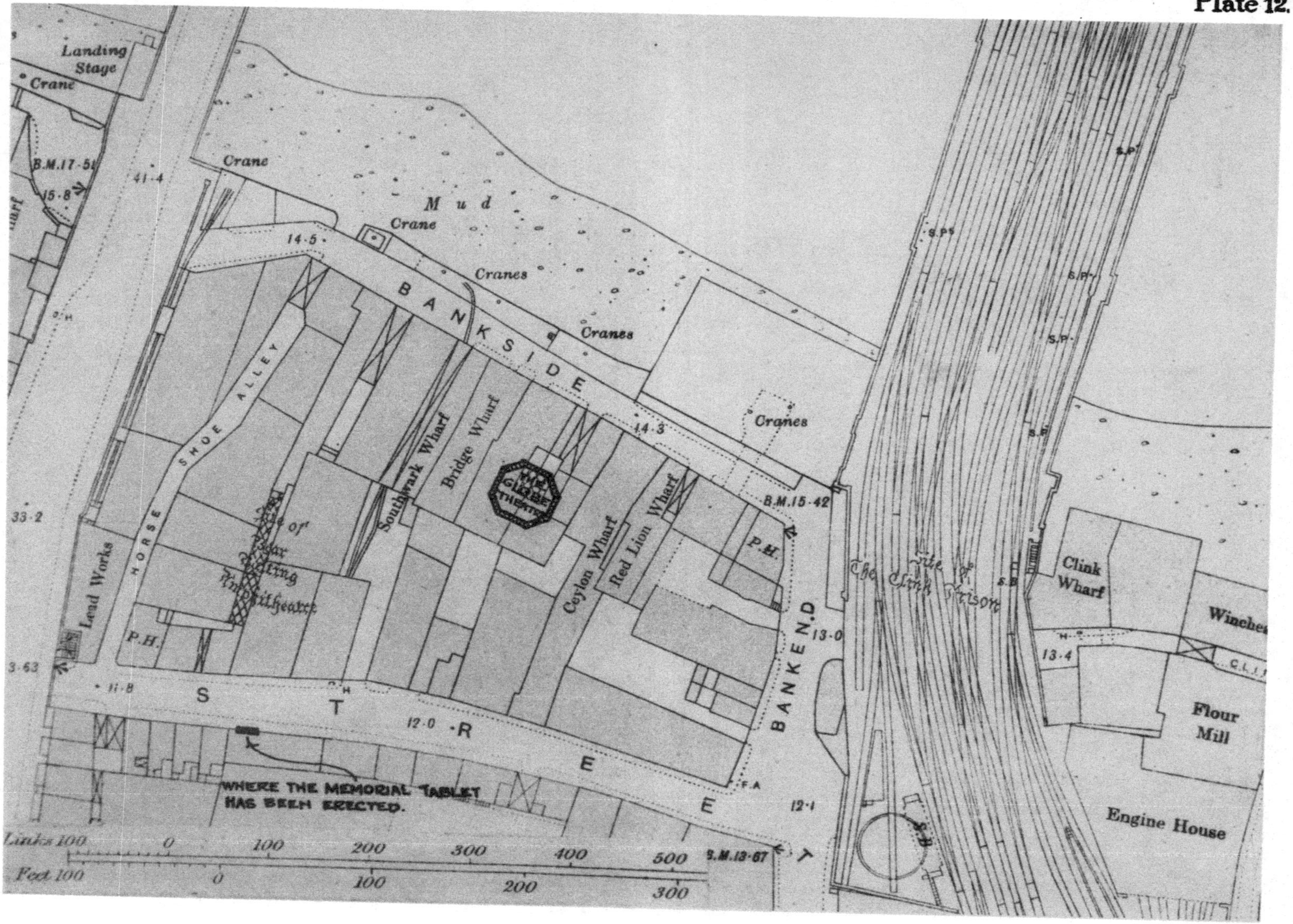

Plate 12.

Site of the Globe Playhouse:
drawn on Ordnance Survey Plan, edⁿ 1917.

Printed in the United States
By Bookmasters